Restoration

Kimberly Miller

BookLeaf Publishing

India | USA | UK

Presentation by *BookLeaf Publishing*

Web: www.bookleafpub.com

E-mail: info@bookleafpub.com

ISBN: 9789358316889

First edition 2024

DEDICATION

To the countless people who have told me that I should publish my poems, this is for all of you.

ACKNOWLEDGEMENT

This book would not be possible without the Lord. I would like to thank my friend, Ben, for going on this journey of faith and poetry with me. Psalms 126:1-3

PREFACE

In Romans it is written, "for all have sinned and fall short of the glory of God, and all are justified freely by his grace through the redemption that came by Christ Jesus" (3:23-24). Yet when individuals fall short, too often condemnation and punishment follow long after one is reconciled to God.

How does one even begin the journey toward reconciliation when all is broken? Clearly, forgiveness is a first step but that does not restore nor does it rebuild. Jesus models agape love for us in that He loved us in our brokenness when we could not love him. Jesus leaves us a new command for us to love our neighbor as ourselves and to pray for our enemies.

So, what if we really took Jesus at his word? What if we really allowed ourselves to love those who hurt us and those whom we have hurt? To let go of the pride and our insistence on being "right"? How would reconciliation really play out in our hearts and lives?

This anthology of poems are my answers to these questions. My prayer is that they resonate

with you in your situation as you seek out
restoration.

Cracked

We are all broken vessels,
cracked beyond all repair,
having little to offer
our chaos causing despair

What we need most we can't see;
what we want most we don't do
Our brokenness is downward spiral,
rotting out everything through and through

We may see the need for a savior
when our lives are a simmering mess
It often takes problem beyond us
to realize that God really knows best

If we don't see we're part of the problem,
or if we aren't in the pit of despair,
we easily judge our neighbor
We are willing to leave him out there

Away from the love of the savior,
out of our community
because she should have known better,
and we are better, you see

There is no hope of reconciliation
even if forgiveness is bestowed
We have lost our way back to restoration;
we have blocked off that road

Because we ignore our own issues
and the sin that weighs us down
We prefer to be better than others
pride blocks mercy, I've found

I know that Jesus won't leave us
He showed mercy to all
The church needs His restoration
to patch up the broken who fall

I beg you to heed my warning;
I urge you to consider my call
Those who judge the most harshly
are the most likely to fall
2 Corinthians 13:11

The dangers of double negatives

Don't think for a minute that I haven't been a mess
That your actions had no fall out
That they didn't cause distress

Don't think for a minute that I am not wounded still
That your hatred of my presence
Has not left a soul-deep chasm to fill

Don't think for a minute that I haven't paid a price
That forgiveness isn't difficult
That the process was somehow nice

Don't think that for a minute that the Lord is done with us
That I haven't tried to walk away
That the Lord hasn't pitched a fuss

Don't think for a minute that God doesn't require more
That He'll let you off the hook
That He will let me settle the score

Don't think for a minute that I am not your friend
That your value isn't innumerable
That God's radical love won't win out in the end
Proverbs 16:2

The folly of anger

I didn't know that I could hurt you
Not in the same way you hurt me
I know that this might seem untrue
But love's opposite is apathy

Assumptions might be okay
When things are going fine
But on a stormy day
Assumptions seem all mine

Hatred really is a perverted love
Strife twists feelings, causing fear
Like a nuclear disaster from above
Its fallout making everything unclear

How was I to know beyond the distant eyes
That you were feeling abandoned too
That I was not despised
But would be welcomed by you?

We both share equal blame on this
The spirit says that's true
The onus on me's a diss
Because you felt the pain too

Avoiding one another
Never catching each other's eyes
Pain should have been a clue this behavior was
despised
Each of us caught in a web of Satan's lies

If I had known you were my brother and friend
I would have had a lot to say
I couldn't have played pretend
And let hurt eat us both away

The evil one attacks those who scare him most
And we listened to his lies
We ignored the Holy Ghost
We, with Lord's anointing, watched our boat
capsize.

Our Father uses the foolish to shame the wise
And that describes the pair of us
Needing restoration of such improbable size
That He gets all glory because it clearly isn't us.
Ecclesiastes 7:9

Hats

There's a difference
between a hat and a mask
the truth and an act

The hat, a mindset,
a rubric of behavior
means to separate

There's a need for space,
a shield to ward off the hurt,
a way to stay sane

A mask subverts all,
allowing one's eyes to hide
You, unseen behind

People can't judge you
if they only know the act,
the part that you play

Masks can block the air,
make it hard to clearly see,
they're suffocating

The message of God
requires we speak with love and
authenticity

Jesus taught his friends,
even though they weren't perfect,
He loved each of them

Let me be very clear,
even He was selective
discernment is key

The growth in your heart
will be much clearer to see
just using the hat
1 Corinthians 13:12

Stand firm

The now and not yet
is the hardest place to be,
we are not where we were
but where we are we've yet to see

It requires discipline
to just stand firm and trust
when we're standing on our own
yet from faith to faith we must

You required nonsense of Noah
to build a boat on the dry land
The butt of jokes for all
until rain fell, as You had planned

You required all from Abraham
when he agreed to follow you
walking in the wilderness; the sacrifice of Issac,
trusting Your process as he was called to

You required courage from Daniel
Your law inscribed on his heart
he refused to be defiled
standing alone until You proved him smart

In fact, this process repeats
throughout history
means that there is purpose in the waiting
one should embrace God's mystery
Galatians 5:1

The darkness

The darkness in a believer's heart
is a necessary thing,
without struggle we wouldn't need to
cling

to the heart of God,
using our meager faith to learn to walk
becoming reliant on our Rock.

The Lord allows us to turn away,
He gives us room to fail,
but He only does this for His light to prevail.

When we commit our lives to Jesus,
we are yoked to His will.
As much as we try to run we are still

tethered to the Lord,
with a cord that will never break.
Our rebellion is an illusion as we can never
shake

Jesus from our hearts,
where He ever changes us.
There is no place of darkness where He is not
enough.

Even the places that are hard to reach,
He leaves nothing unexposed,
there is no part of us we can permanently close.

God compels our hearts toward Him;
I don't think we have a choice.
He's working on our strongholds and for that we
should rejoice.
1 John 1:5-7

Not safe for church

Lord, I want to follow you
Despite the sh*t you put me through
Demanding time upon my knees
To teach me some humility

Pushing common sense aside
Leaving only tatters of my pride
This is the way You work in me
Which bites the big one because I see

All the ways I have been blind
When I thought I was doing fine
Why do you always require more of me
Then anyone else in my family?

I know I am a hard-headed one
Opinionated sometimes just for fun
Sometimes it seems I serve you best
When my mind gets little rest

I really think this is absurd
That you only want to share Your word
When I should be fast asleep
I'm pretty sure these lessons could keep

For the hours I am awake
In the time that I attempt to make
But I guess my efforts are in vain
So I trust in you to keep me sane
Psalms 55:17

Breadcrumbs

Lord, just a thank you
for the faith I hardly see
the tiny breadcrumbs,

the kernels of faith,
that You reveal to me from
only a distance

Things You have me do
that I fail to understand
never return void

They appear again
when the way's very obscured
They are not consumed

Little mementos
that prove you've been by my side,
leading where I go

Sometimes it is hard
you forget where you have been
trekking wilderness

But You remind me
of the path I've walked by faith
walking hand-in-hand

And that gives me hope
for the future yet obscured
as we journey on …
Hebrews 11:1

Let the fur fly

Being a Christian
is sometimes masochistic
as you fight yourself

You find the concepts
of grace and mercy are hard
and don't satisfy

They're an annoyance
like cat fur that permeates
and clings everywhere

Infecting things never
even exposed to the source.
Contaminated

Cat fur is like Grace,
it diffuses everywhere,
showing Your mercy

Trying to prevent
the fur from flying around
is impossible

So it is with Grace,
the Lord beats you down until
His mercy infects

the grudges you hold,
when you have no intention
of letting them go

The Lord and His grace
are extremely annoying
when you are still mad
James 4:6

Fault lines

We all have fault lines in our lives
Areas of hardship and doubt
Invisible caverns of instability
That seem gone until a strong bout

A storm rumbles into our lives
And then the fault lines all give way
All that we have built will crumble
Our works will melt away

We are left with nothing
But the things we have built on your rock
All other things are in pieces
And we are left in shock

How could all our good works
Be dashed like sandcastles by waves?
Because we are nothing without You
Only things built in You are saved.
Luke 6:48-49

Strongholds

Someone prayed for me,
for patience, of all things,
The Lord giggled with glee
as He watched the havoc that brings

He showed me the strongholds in my life
like I had nothing to work on
As if my life was devoid of strife
and my impatience was somehow gone

But that didn't really didn't matter,
He found the things I most despise
and said the strongholds need to shatter,
not mastering small things makes me unwise

How can I trust the Lord for big things,
if the small things master me?
My progress tangled up and tiptoeing
yet I expect from others, growth abundantly

The tasks I most despise
are giving me perspective,
forcing me to look from another's eyes
I realize my impatience is ineffective

The strongholds seem too much to master
only when we view them from below,
from God's perspective it is not such a disaster,
grace and wisdom for the challenge He will
bestow
2 Corinthians 10:4

Hesed

God's economy
of grace is difficult to
grasp, even as it
works and changes all of us
from enemies to brothers

The same hand that hurt
and used his sword against you (John 18:10)
will be used to heal (Acts 3:6)
The liar that denied you (Luke 22:61)
will end up loving you most (John 21:17)

The most zealously
opposed to you will end up
blinded on the road, (Acts 9:8)
waiting for your touch of grace
Us showing him your mercy (Acts 9:15)

The most religious
can get caught up in the law,
causing division
until you reveal your Grace
and how the law has no place (Acts 10:15)

It's superseded
by love's economy that
heals the deepest pains
because love always expands
and erases all our flaws (John 13:34)

Repartee

Everytime I think I understand
what the Lord is doing,
His intentions are never what I planned
and I relearn how limited my viewing

Why do I ever think that I can fully see
the grandness of His plans?
When what the Lord is requiring of me
I often fail to understand

I find this lack of vision frustrating;
this seems to amuse the Lord
He doesn't seem to object to us debating
But it's idiocy: I've never even scored

Yet, I find His instruction annoying
It seems He could be more clear,
but the Lord seems to be enjoying
Our repartee, but this may shock those who
think Him austere
Phillipians 4:4

Discipline

The Lord's correction
Can either be the carrot
Or his Shepherd's crook

A crook sounds so kind
But it really is a stick
A forceful means to

Shove me from folly,
From the crevice or ledge as
I find myself stuck

The Lord is more kind
To other folk offering
His carrot of grace

A sweet incentive
To feel His agape love
And choose to follow

But with me it seems
He always uses the stick
Until I learn grace
Titus 2:11-12

The sidelines

Lord, you are in charge
I step aside waiting for
You to intervene

And yet You do not
my universe collapses
and leaves me broken

And yet I know that
Your promises never fail
This is not the end

Sometimes broken is
the only path to being
completely restored

He won't let me sit
waiting for someone else to
go where I've been called

I am changed to fit,
master the situation,
so truth prevails
Romans 8:28

The anatomy of hate

Hate is like using the spine of a knife
You have to jab it deep
To stab another's life

It is an act done in darkness
Completely devoid of love
Viewing in black and white starkness

Damaging another
Is intended when you respond in fear
It becomes hard to see "other" as brother

It allows a chasm of pain
Where grace can never touch
You cannot show love to one you disdain

When people are invisible
Behind the screen of "other"
They are easily divisible

This anatomy of hate
We act as judge and jury
And easily alienate

But while hate has gained the upper hand
Love will overcome
God's grace for us will never let this stand

You may not see how love could win your war
But there is nothing God can't change
It might even be your heart learning to love
more
Leviticus 19:18

Turbulence

Crying for no reason
at least none I understand,
today's not worse than yesterday
it is just everything is too much.
It is like one more person suffering
has put me over the ledge;
I have nothing left to give.

I am tired of convincing myself
that everything is fine;
that all will be well if I just give things more
time.
At heart I am tired of trying to prove myself
like I am somehow unworthy,
but I can't let them see me
broken.
Psalms 73:26

The journey to joy

To find peace you must
use the shoes of the gospel
and go where you're sent

Hurts will be mended
when we forgive from the heart
as we trust in You

Our love is a mere
reflection, we must seek out
the Son's love for us

The only way to
become perfected is to
learn to walk in love

Unity can spring
up like a flower from the
cesspool we have made

Bringing a new joy
to our hearts, we are transformed,
our spirit is changed

Others will see Your
reflected love in our eyes
Your fullness of joy
Psalms 19:8

Clothed in righteousness

What the Lord destroys,
He creates again
Sometimes only from the flames
new life is attained

While the flames destroy,
bitterness and tears,
it is an acrid thing
as the old disappears

Just like a forest fire
consuming acres in a night,
we are powerless,
yet still we fight

But fire purifies
renewing our hearts and minds,
bringing forth new life again,
a rebirth before our eyes

So when your world's in ash,
when destruction reigns,
remember God uses fire
It is not in vain

Sometimes His spirit in fire
requires new space
to work in our lives
as we're rebuilt through grace
Matthew 6:30

Love's energy

Love is not like pie
It is not consumed
It has no serving size

Love cannot be earned
There's nothing you can do
to lose or gain it

Like the laws of energy
Love only has two states
Active and potential

God's kinetic love
has a power of its own
that calls us into action

Love cannot stay passive
or waiting very long
God creates the potential

And then like dominoes we fall
into divine appointments
that require active love

We might wonder where
this love comes from
but there always is enough

God's infinite love
moves our hearts
to go
1 John 3:18

In review

Even though this situation
has been one of the hardest in my life,
I'm not sure I would change it
and eliminate the strife.

What I've learned has value,
and to eliminate the bad,
leaves us back at zero
negating the growth we've had.

Clearly there were issues
and perhaps we're not all through,
but knowing the God of me
is the God of you,

makes me pretty confident
that He'll never be done with us.
He will find a way to fix
whatever He must.

He's doing a new thing,
which couldn't have occurred
if things had just continued.
This way God has the final word.

So I guess I wouldn't change things,
even if I could.
As what God is doing amazes me,
His purpose is clearly for our good.
Isaiah 43:19

9 789358 316889